W9-BPQ-587

Reasons To Vote For Democrats

A Comprehensive Guide

By
Michael J. Knowles

I have written my work, not as an essay which is to win the applause of the moment, but as a possession for all time.

—Thucydides

Table of Contents

Chapter 1
Economics

Reasons To Vote For Democrats

Reasons To Vote For Democrats

Chapter 2
Foreign Policy

Reasons To Vote For Democrats

Reasons To Vote For Democrats

Chapter 3
Civil Rights

Reasons To Vote For Democrats

45

Chapter 4
Education

Reasons To Vote For Democrats

Chapter 5
Homeland Security

Chapter 6
Energy

Chapter 7
Jobs

Chapter 8
Crime

Reasons To Vote For Democrats

Chapter 9
Immigration

.

Reasons To Vote For Democrats

Reasons To Vote For Democrats

Reasons To Vote For Democrats

Chapter 10
Values and Principles

Reasons To Vote For Democrats

226

Reasons To Vote For Democrats

231

Reasons To Vote For Democrats

Reasons To Vote For Democrats

Bibliography

Alinsky, Saul. *Rules for Radicals: A Pragmatic Primer for Realistic Radicals*. New York: Vintage, 1971.

Berg, A. Scott. *Wilson*. New York: Berkley Books, 2014.

Bernstein, Carl. *A Woman In Charge: The Life of Hillary Rodham Clinton*. London: Vintage, 2008.

Black, Edwin. *War Against The Weak: Eugenics and America's Campaign to Create a Master Race*. New York: Dialog Press, 2012.

Blight, David. *Race and Reunion: The Civil War in American Memory*. Cambridge: Belknap, 2002.

Bourne, Peter G. *Jimmy Carter: A Comprehensive Biography from Plains to Post-Presidency*. New York: Scriber, 1997.

Brackett, Elizabeth. *Pay to Play: How Rod Blagojevich Turned Political Corruption into a National Sideshow*. Lanham: Ivan R. Dee, 2009.

Brands, H.W. *Reagan: The Life*. New York: Anchor, 2016.

Bullard, Sara. *The Ku Klux Klan: A History of Racism & Violence*. Darby: Diane Publishing Co., 1996.

Byrd, Robert C. *Robert C. Byrd: Child of the Appalachian Coalfields*. Morgantown: West Virginia University Press, 2005.

Caro, Robert. *Master of the Senate*. London: Vintage, 2003.

------. *Means of Ascent*. London: Vintage, 1991.

------. *The Passage of Power*. London: Vintage, 2013.

------. *The Path to Power*. London: Vintage, 1990.

Catton, Bruce. *A Stillness at Appomattox*. New York: Anchor, 1953.

------. *Mr. Lincoln's Army*. New York: Anchor, 1990.

------. *The Centennial History of the Civil War, 1861-65*. New York: Doubleday, 1961.

Chesterton, Gilbert Keith. *Eugenics and Other Evils*. London: Cassell and Company, 1922.

Clements, Kendrick A. *The Presidency of Woodrow Wilson*. Lawrence: University Press of Kansas, 1992.

Cooper, John Milton. *Woodrow Wilson: A Biography*. London: Vintage, 2011.

Creighton, Margaret. *The Colors of Courage: Gettysburg's Forgotten History – Immigrants, Women, and African Americans in the Civil War's Defining Battle*. New York: Basic Books, 2006.

Dallek, Robert. *Lyndon B. Johnson: Portrait of a President*. Oxford: Oxford University Press, 2004.

Damore, Leo. *Senatorial Privilege: The Chappaquiddick Cover-up*. Washington, D.C.: Regnery Publishing, 1988.

Fahs, Alice. *The Imagined Civil War: Popular Literature of the North & South, 1861-1865*. Chapel Hill: University of North Carolina Press, 2003.

Faust, Drew Gilpin. *This Republic of Suffering: Death and the American Civil War*. London: Vintage Press, 2009.

Fehrenbacher, Don. *The Dred Scott Case: Its Significance in American Law and Politics*. Oxford: Oxford University Press, 2001.

Fitzgerald, Michael. *Urban Emancipation: Popular Politics in Reconstruction Mobile, 1860-1890*. Baton Rouge: Louisiana State University Press, 2002.

Foner, Eric. *A Short History of Reconstruction*. New York: Harper Perennial, 2015.

Foote, Shelby. *The Civil War: A Narrative*. New York: Vintage Books, 1986.

Gettys, Embry Martin. *A History of the Democratic Party in Congress from 1897 to 1905*. Leland Stanford Junior University, 1932.

Grant, George. *Killer Angel: A Biography of Planned Parenthood's Margaret Sanger*. Nashville: Cumberland House Publishing, 2001.

Guelzo, Allen C. *Abraham Lincoln: Redeemer President*. Grand Rapids, Eerdmans, 2002.

Hahn, Steven. *A Nation Under Our Feet: Black Political Struggles in the Rural South from Slavery to the Great Migration*. Cambridge: Belknap, 2005.

Harris, William C. *With Charity For All: Lincoln and the Restoration of the Union*. Lexington: University Press of Kentucky, 1999.

Hazlitt, Henry. *Economics In One Lesson: The Shortest and Surest Way to Understand Basic Economics*. New York: Crown Publishing, 1959.

Holt, Michael. *The Rise and Fall of the American Whig Party: Jacksonian Politics and the Onset of the Civil War*. Oxford: Oxford University Press, 1999.

Leonard, Thomas C. *Illiberal Reformers: Race, Eugenics, and American Economics in the Progressive Era*. Princeton: Princeton University Press, 2017.

McGlone, Robert. *John Brown's War Against Slavery*. Cambridge: Cambridge University Press, 2009.

McPherson, James. *For Cause and Comrades: Why Men Fought in the Civil War*. Oxford: Oxford University Press, 1998.

Moynihan, Daniel Patrick. *The Negro Family: A Case for National Action*. Washington, D.C.: U.S. Department of Labor, 1965.

Neubeck, Kenneth J. and Noel A. Cazenave. *Welfare Racism: Playing the Race Card Against America's Poor*. Abringdon-on-Thames: Routledge, 2001.

Nelson, Donald Frederick. *Chappaquiddick Tragedy: Kennedy's Second Passenger Revealed*. Gretna: Pelican, 2016.

Nevins, Allan. *Ordeal of the Union*. New York: Collier, 1992.

------. *The Emergence of Lincoln*. New York: Scribner's, 1950.

------. *The War for the Union*. New York: Scribner's, 1971.

Pestritto, Ronald J. *Woodrow Wilson and the Roots of Modern Liberalism*. Lanham: Rowman & Littlefield, 2005.

Peterson, David J. *Revoking the Moral Order: The Ideology of Positivism and the Vienna Circle*. Lanham: Lexington Books, 1999.

Potter, David M. *The Impending Crisis*. New York: Harper Perennial, 2011.

Price, Joann F. *Barack Obama: A Biography*. Santa Barbara: Greenwood, 2008.

Rable, George C. *Fredericksburg! Fredericksburg!* Chapel Hill: University of North Carolina Press, 2012.

Richardson, Heather Cox. *To Make Men Free: A History of the Republican Party*. New York: Basic Books, 2014.

Roberts, Russell. *A History of the Democratic Party*. Hallandale: Mitchell Lane Publishers, 2012.

Royko, Mike. *Boss: Richard J. Daley of Chicago*. New York: Plume, 1988.

Sanger, Margaret. *Woman and the New Race*. Elkhart: Truth Publishing Company, 1921.

Schweizer, Peter. *Clinton Cash: The Untold Story of How and Why Foreign Governments and Businesses Helped Make Bill and Hillary Rich*. New York: Harper Collins, 2016.

Selfa, Lance. *The Democrats: A Critical History*. New York: Haymarket Books, 2012.

Sieracki, Bernard. *A Just Cause: The Impeachment and Removal of Governor Rod Blagojevich*. Carbondale: Southern Illinois University Press, 2015.

Stampp, Kenneth. *The Peculiar Institution*. London: Vintage Press, 1989.

Stout, Harry S. *Upon the Altar of the Nation: A Moral History of the Civil War*. London: Penguin Books, 2007.

Summers, Mark Wahlgren. *A Dangerous Stir: Fear, Paranoia, and the Making of Reconstruction*. Chapel Hill: University of North Carolina Press, 2014.

Tedrow, Richard L. and Thomas L. Tedrow. *Death at Chappaquiddick*. Gretna: Pelican, 1980.

Wade, Wyn Craig. *The Fiery Cross: The Ku Klux Klan in America*. Oxford: Oxford University Press, 1998.

Walsh, Michael. *The People v. the Democratic Party*. New York: Encounter Books, 2012.

Wiley, Bell Irvin. *The Life of Billy Yank*. Baton Rouge: Louisiana State University Press, 2008.

------. *The Life of Johnny Reb*. Baton Rouge: Louisiana State University Press, 2008.

Wormser, Richard. *The Rise and Fall of Jim Crow*. New
York: St. Martin's Press, 2003.

41422605R00149

Made in the USA
Middletown, DE
11 March 2017